D0788126

USING MAGNETS

By Nora Roman

Gareth Stevens
PUBLISHING

Please visit our website, www.garethstevens.com. For a free color catalog of all our high-quality books, call toll free 1-800-542-2595 or fax 1-877-542-2596.

Cataloging-in-Publication Data

Names: Roman, Nora.
Title: Using magnets / Nora Roman.
Description: New York : Gareth Stevens Publishing, 2018. | Series: Super science tools | Includes index.
Identifiers: ISBN 9781482463934 (pbk.) | ISBN 9781482463958 (library bound) | ISBN 9781482463941 (6 pack)
Subjects: LCSH: Magnets–Juvenile literature. | Magnetic fields–Juvenile literature.
Classification: LCC QC757.R66 2018 | DDC 538–dc23

Published in 2018 by
Gareth Stevens Publishing
111 East 14th Street, Suite 349
New York, NY 10003

Copyright © 2018 Gareth Stevens Publishing

Designer: Laura Bowen
Editor: Therese Shea

Photo credits: Cover, p. 1 Rubberball/Mike Kemp/Shutterstock.com; pp. 1–24 (series art) T.Sumaetho/Shutterstock.com; p. 5 antos777/Shutterstock.com; p. 7 Jakinnboaz/Shutterstock.com; p. 9 NoPainNoGain/Shutterstock.com; p. 11 (top) Pat_Hastings/Shutterstock.com; p. 11 (bottom) supersaiyan3/Shutterstock.com; p. 13 (cobalt) farbled/Shutterstock.com; p. 13 (iron) Fokin Oleg/Shutterstock.com; p. 13 (nickel) Alchemist-hp/Shutterstock.com; p. 13 (magnetite) Aleksandr Pobedimskiy/Shutterstock.com; p. 15 (compass) Feng Yu/Shutterstock.com; p. 15 (Earth) Snowbelle/Shutterstock.com; p. 17 marekusz/Shutterstock.com; p. 19 SpeedKingz/Shutterstock.com; p. 21 (girl) Rubberball/Mike Kemp/Getty Images; p. 21 (magnets) GOLFX/Shutterstock.com; p. 21 (notebook) Raihana Asral/Shutterstock.com.

Printed in the United States of America

CPSIA compliance information: Batch #CS17GS: For further information contact Gareth Stevens, New York, New York at 1-800-542-2595.

CONTENTS

Boldface words appear in the glossary.

Magnets, Not Magic

Magnets can push and pull things—without even touching them! They can also stick to some objects. You probably have toys that are magnets. Magnets are also important tools. Magnets *aren't* magic. So how do they work?

In the Field

All magnets are made of special **metals**. Even rocks that have bits of special metal in them can act as magnets. The metals have a magnetic field. That's the area around them in which their force can work.

Magnetic Fields

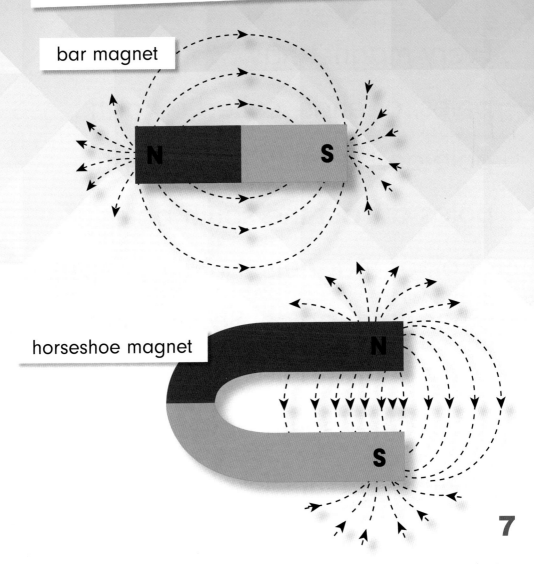

bar magnet

horseshoe magnet

Every magnet has two opposite poles, or ends, called a north pole and a south pole. North poles **attract** the south poles of other magnets, but they **repel** other north poles. South poles attract north poles, but they repel other south poles.

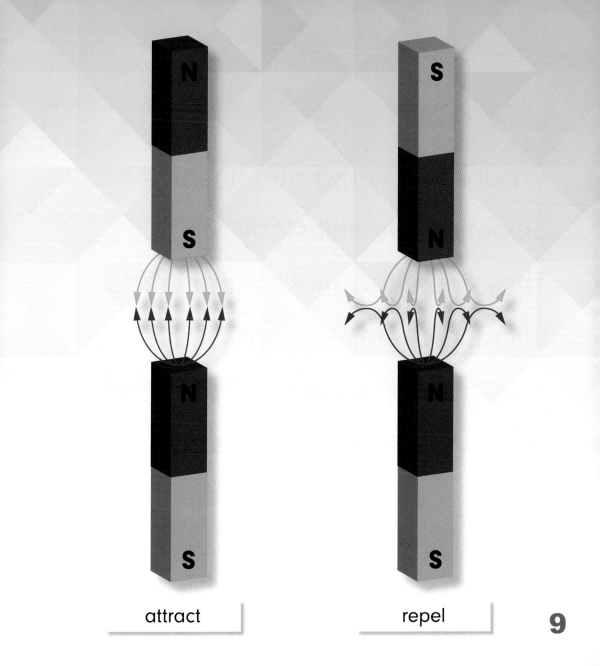

attract

repel

9

What gives a magnet its force? Scientists are still studying that! They know magnetism has to do with the **atoms** that make up matter. They think parts of atoms called electrons act a certain way that creates a magnetic field.

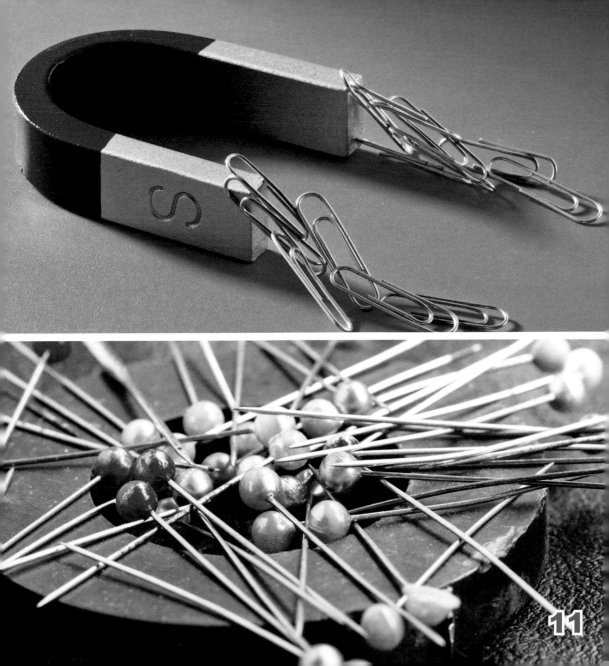

11

Magnetic Matter

Lodestone is a rock that is a **permanent** magnet. Some matter becomes a **temporary** magnet when it's touching another magnet. Iron, nickel, and cobalt are metals used to make temporary magnets. Some matter, such as wood, is never magnetic.

cobalt

nickel

iron

lodestone

13

Pointing the Way

Magnets can help you find your way. A compass contains a magnetic needle. It points north because Earth acts as a magnet, too! The poles of the compass needle are attracted to—and point at—the opposite poles of Earth's magnetic field.

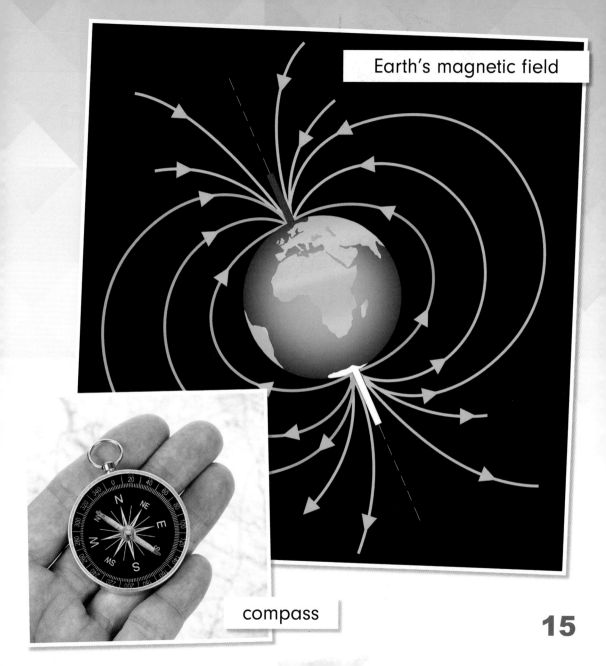

Earth's magnetic field

compass

15

Electromagnets All Around

Scientists use **electricity** to make temporary magnets. When an electric **current** flows through a wire, it creates a magnetic field. When the wire is wrapped around a metal such as iron, the object becomes an electromagnet. Electromagnets are used in **motors**.

17

Electromagnets are in so many objects and tools we use every day. We often don't even realize how many. Without electromagnets, we wouldn't have computers, refrigerators, or even cars! They also help make pictures of the inside of our bodies.

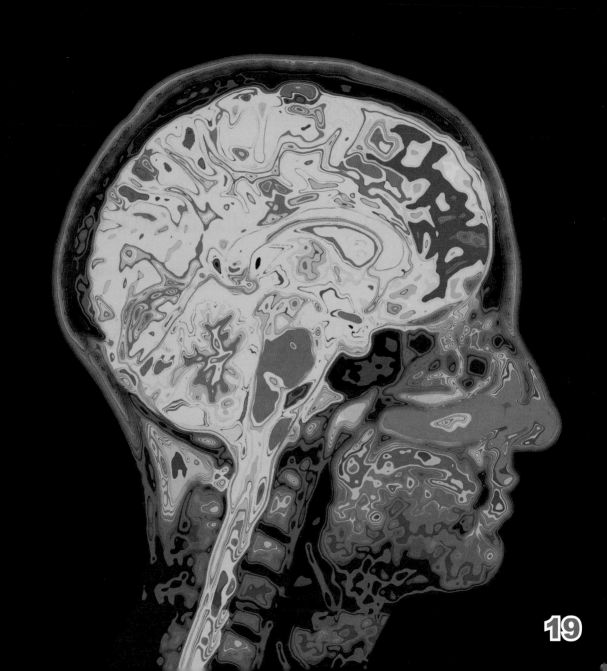

19

Thank You, Magnets!

We're so lucky Earth has natural magnets. We're also lucky that scientists have made **inventions** that use magnets. Maybe someday you'll be a scientist who works with magnets, too. What invention using magnets would you make?

You Use Magnets!

1) Use a magnet around the house.

2) Draw pictures of three magnetic objects you find.

21

GLOSSARY

atom: one of the smallest bits of matter

attract: to draw nearer

current: a flow of electricity

electricity: energy that is carried through wires and is used to operate machines

invention: a tool created after study

metal: a shiny rock, like iron or gold, found in the ground

motor: a machine that produces motion or power for doing work

permanent: unchanging

repel: to push away

temporary: lasting for a limited time

FOR MORE INFORMATION

BOOKS

Branley, Franklyn M. *What Makes a Magnet?* New York, NY: Harper, 2016.

Jennings, Terry. *Magnets.* Mankato, MN: Smart Apple Media, 2009.

Silverman, Buffy. *Magnet Power.* North Mankato, MN: Rourke Publishing, 2012.

WEBSITES

Electromagnetism and Electric Motors
www.ducksters.com/science/physics/electromagnetism_and_electric_motors.php
Learn more about how electricity and magnetism work together.

Magnetism
www.explainthatstuff.com/magnetism.html
Read all about magnets and magnetism.

INDEX